T0015270

CALL ME
EXILE

CALL ME
EXILE

AARON BROWN

STEPHEN F. AUSTIN STATE UNIVERSITY PRESS

Copyright © 2022 Stephen F. Austin State University Press

All rights reserved. This book or any portion thereof may not be
reproduced or used in any manner whatsoever without the express written
permission of the publisher.

Project Manager: Kimberly Verhines
Book Design by Cierra Krause

Cover Photo: Golden Route, 1982
Etching with gold ink on grey handmade paper
Dimensions: 30 x 22.5 inches
Image: © Zarina; Courtesy of Zarina's Studio

ISBN: 978-1-62288-241-0
First Edition

for my children

ACKNOWLEDGMENTS

"Abecedarian" and "In a parallel universe," in *Collateral*. "After You Left," "Dreaming in Arabic," and "A Thousand Ways You've Wounded," in *Prairie Schooner*. "Always We Begin Again" and "Twig-Weaving" in *EcoTheo Review*. "Beatific Vision" in *jmww*. "Beqaa Valley, Lebanon" in *Michigan Quarterly Review*. "Bury" in *Rock & Sling*. "Cable Guy" in *Ink & Letters*. "Call Me Exile" in *Consequence*. "Christ in the Suburbs" in *Presence*. "Death is the Door" in *Bearings online*. "God of the Midwest" in *Image*. "God Particle" in *Windhover*. "How We Come to Language" and "Poem" in *Reformed Journal*. "Hymn" in *Relief*. "Old Man Watching Dunkirk" in *Rattle online*. "Origins" in *Burningword*. "The Pastor Walks Me Through His House" in *Fare Forward*. "Suspension of (Dis)belief" and "Disappearance" (published as "Grief") in *The Cresset*. "To the Stars Through Difficulty" in *Valparaiso Poetry Review*. "Via Negativa" in *Ruminate*. "What the Therapist Says" in *Christian Century*.

For their support during the writing of this book, I would also like to thank the Collegeville Institute, *Image's* Glen Workshops, Sterling College, and LeTourneau University. Unending gratitude to the members of the Longview poetry writing group, among whom include Ellis Purdie, Amy Carpenter, Lila Robinett, Amanda Martinez Beck, and Randall Compton. To others whose insight have influenced these poems--Michael Collier, Lisa Fay Coutley, Hala Alyan, Siobhan Scarry, Li-Young Lee, Stanley Plumly, Nathaniel Lee Hansen—thank you.

TABLE OF CONTENTS

Acknowledgments

III

He fills life but no one sees him. He turns life into foam and plunges into it. He turns tomorrow into a prey and hopelessly pursues it. His words are engraved in the direction of loss loss loss.

...

I'd have made out of all this for the wound
A song like a spear
Piercing trees, stones and heaven

—Adonis

I

You were born, you had body, you died…
Believe me, I loved you all.

—Gwendolyn Brooks

After You Left

Our dog smells the cloth you used to tuck
under our son as you nursed—she lies

down beside it, sighs, and gives me
the old world look of dogs

as if she knows it will only be
the two of us, left to memory.

What it must be like to smell the past
and future, to smell grief and lie down in it.

Bury

they say if you can't part with something
bury it the way a dog saves a bone
in the earth so you bury all your years your past
life bury whole countries and passports
bury the rainwind bury the friends dead
or alive who used to throw rocks at the dead
cattle skulls on the forest path to the river
bury that river drying up into sand anyways
bury the road where trucks are bullets birthing
dirt clouds bury the plane that took you away
watching your friends standing on the cracked
tarmac bury the whole town its mud walls
glinting tin roofs all buried beneath the soil
of memory
              bury your new life the narrow
streets of dying towns bury your degrees
built on unearthing the past bury your love
and your child bury the messages that come
to you from the buried those who ask you
how is your life how is your life how is
your life bury those messages too in an inbox

What the Therapist Says

The therapist says to *sit with your loneliness*
so I sit in the middle of my apartment,
walls of boxes around me, clothes
still lodged in trashbags two months in.
I think of how everything is a metaphor
for acceptance. *Brush past the feeling*
but do not face it yet. The therapist tells me
that everything is a repetition, but I take it
to mean that every minute is a chance
to relive losing. So I practice driving
slower than the speed limit, letting
the night enter through the open windows.
I practice finding a booth at the restaurant,
being the only one to order, eat, and clear.
I practice walking in the dark
when I take out my dog, husks of cicadas
casting shadows along the stucco.
Everything a practice of disappearance:
beyond the streetlight the road knows
no division with night, even the molted
skin of the cicada is a sign
that there was once a body.

Twig-Weaving

I was gone when the wind took the nest
gone when the broom handle fell

gone when the circled twigs and mud
came down—this time gone, scattered

across pavement, gone the life inside—
gone the egg came rolling, came cracking,

gone bird yoke spreading just like guilt

gone their little offering of home
gone the birds will try again

gone we will not stop their twig-weaving
gone their woven womb.

Disappearance

At the riverbank, beneath the bridge, a child plays in the saltgrass,
    sifts his hands through stem, laughing as if chasing

a frog through the brush. You do not want the child to know you
    are watching. You do not want the child to see

you longing for his happiness. This visible riverbed,
    this bridge built like a tipped wall. What you see is given

to you only as the dawn fog recedes. Along the guardrails of the
    bridge, the fog leaves behind its icy encasement.

A bird left by the V's flying south cries in the wind's wake.
    The snow will melt and swell the creek until

there will be no riverbed, no place for the child to play,
    and no child either—imagined ghost, glimpsed then gone.

Another

Some other mother
strolling another
boy whose face
appears over
the frame
to stare at my
missed jumpshots
before his vision
is overtaken
by the pond
just down the hill
where he gets out
sapling stumpy
legs wobbling
as his mother
snaps a portrait
for the future
a portrait
where always
in the water's
warped surface
I am there
and I am not.

Via Negativa

You are not the wind scraping branch on pane
or the continental plate strike-slipping beneath
a valley of bones drought-brittled and baked.
You are not hurricane clouds circling around
an ever-turning eye, slow-moving and a mile
wide, surrounding surging sea, framing bound
the heaving-heavens looking down on swirling
earth—nor are you the grass-fire spread before
the rains come cooling brush, keeping
calm what you are not. But maybe you are
somewhere close, not the land but the dust,
not the sea but the wind making waves or
the deep-dark pull of lunar longing, wanting
the vastness between us shrunk to nothing.

Christat in the Suburbs, **Oil on Canvas, 1920-1924, Roualt**

Is it enough
you don't stay up

that I pass by

and in this alley
meet only

the least of these?

You'll be driving
some road home

from work from

picking up your child
or your groceries—

I'll be here

here in the stucco
home suburbs

beneath expanding

night treading
the stone way

unshod motioning

my lost children
into the oblivion

of a lightless street.

Death is the Door

Death is the door that never closes
on the slow life hours, expectation budding,

always a light ray streaming
into an empty room.

Some days are days for the dying:
the Sunday silence, the Monday mourning.

The task then is to wait for illumination:

the Sunday silence, the Monday mourning,
some days are days for the dying

into an empty room
always a light ray streaming

on the slow life hours, expectation budding—
death is the door that never closes.

Split

Here in the night the rain hits
the window like tears,

lights from other distant rooms
bleed through the wet.

This: the first sweet second
I am alone, even when it's still

me and the camera in the corner,
me and the doctors at their screens

making sure I don't kill myself.
I don't know what to think

except to think, what to pray
except to pray. When in the common

room I play a few piano notes,
the other patients tell me not

to stop. They don't know this has all been
my song to you. They don't know

my mind is split down to my heart.
They don't see me each night

at the window, standing at the edge
of the world, calling to you.

II

Maybe language and grief are like night and day, they pass each other mostly, and if you can just get close so that the tips of morning and night touch even for a second, that would be incredible.

—Victoria Chang

In a parallel universe

you never left / your friends
never died / your ears never heard
the gunshot never fired / the smoke
never rose / your C-130 never winged
its way out / you never lived months
waiting to return / in a parallel universe

you stayed / went to university
in the capital / found a job drilling
wells into the earth / searched out
water in the earth's heart / the danger
to your parallel universe not war
but boredom / perhaps
you saved your francs / to build
a brick house out of town / brought
your love to live there / perhaps
you married in the sands / perhaps
your skin changed into the baked
dust color / in a parallel universe

you never know the art
of losing / the loss of loving /
never know when to stop
digging a never-ending well / a well
that never seeps moisture
but is brittle all the way down

Dreaming in Arabic

Do you remember what it was like to dream in Arabic?
Conversations and memories told and retold in Arabic?

The muezzin calls from a distant neighborhood as your father
finishes tea with friends, laughing at a joke told only in Arabic.

The screech of chalk in your mind when you rehearse
your oustaz's lessons, learned your khurufs in Arabic.

You remember the word *akhdar* describes several shades: the color
of a tree's leaves and of its bark, colors limitless in Arabic.

The waking in and out of sleep to hear the beggar boys
on the street chanting their alms prayer in Arabic.

The opening of *l'Equipe* you brought from a plane—
friends debate which team will win it all, all in Arabic.

Your friends visit you here in dreamspace, asking *when will you
be back or can I come visit?* questions that arrive in Arabic.

In the dream, you fill out your immigration card knowing
residence, nationality, destination, and the form is all in Arabic.

On days that you are awake, you try to remember the word
for *life* or *love* or *war*, full of regret for losing your Arabic.

Your name *Haroun* lingers with you in mind and messages, friends
telling you of wives, children, of their lives in Arabic.

Return to the Security Checkpoint for Your Lost Item

You have forgotten your laptop / your pair of shoes
your belt / your toothpaste / your mouthwash
your briefcase / *can we see your ID?*
your backpack / your checked bag
of memories / *what is your final destination?*
your luggage of lost things / your abandoned
country / your new country / *anything to declare?*
the parents who birthed you / the parents
who raised you / the parents who made you
sweet meatsauce sandwiches / *have you been given*
an item by anyone else? / your grandparents
here and abroad / taking pictures
of you / pouring tea for you
forgot your brothers real and unreal
each street an adventure / each tree a tree
to sit under / *what is the purpose*
of your trip? / to talk away the day
by the river / to sit by them as they bend
to pray / your lost brothers / all of them
they come for you / voices on the intercom
saying return and claim us / do not forget us /
please return / return / return.

Call Me Exile

I

Between the condo tower and electronics store,
you were let off—florescent bulbs flooding shadowed road,

cars shuddering in desert winter: January in Amman,
taxi drivers coasting up to coffee shacks, beansteam

fogging glass, cigarettes
embering themselves in drivers' hands.

The first snow fell
around you then, standing in the median.

Wind-whipped between the lanes,
cold beyond belief, you forgot where you were going

then remembered the apartment so cold, at the turn *yemin*—
and the grayblock walls—*hun bas*.

You huddled by a gas burner, slept under five-layers—
city of Hittite towers and no central heating.

When you awoke in the bare room, brother sleeping
beside you, your breath had already become cloud.

II

Returning to a different home: crossing
the Levant on Egypt Air, shahada prayed

as the plane lifts wheels from tarmac
then touching down, a different desert—

the oven-like streets of N'Djamena, mango juice stands
and corner markets selling Nido and noodles—

first they took the water, then the lights,
then the cell towers so that rebels could not

place a call, could not coordinate
an out-maneuver. You were caught

in crossfire, saved by walls you wanted
to scale, climb up out of

bullet-shudder, watch the smoke signal
the end of childhood

signal the middleway of wandering,
adulthood far ahead

or already here, so long passed you didn't
realize it. Faced with the wind

ushered from guns, bullets thudding walls
like taxis breaking over speed-bumps,

you entered the oncoming lane of war—
what fell around you was not snow, but shells.

III

Where are you now? What sand-scraped street
winters in your mind? When you go out

during night's deadest hours, sky so crisp
the constellations open up to you, do you

remember the way each winter was its own struggle
for breath to come warmly,

for breath to be stilled? Like waking, thinking
for a second you are back—

an uncanny second when you mistake
morning birds for bombs.

Abecedarian

You were [a]live [b]efore the [c]rush
of [d]eath—the door through which you
[e]ntered your whole [f]amily [g]one
from this living land. [H]ear the sound
[i]n the absence of sound. The [j]ust
disappeared silence of footsteps quic[k]ening
[l]ike a child's run. [M]ake your way
through the tiled halls, the [n]uminous shadows
at the end, [o]pen the door you find, [p]eeling
back this door to a [q]uiet [r]oom, with nothing in it
but a chair for you to [s]it. [T]rust the smooth s[u]rface
of the [v]eined [w]ood e[x]actly how [y]ou remembered it—
memory so strong you are haunted more than ama[z]ed.

Some other morning

The thunder quiets to a cool
whisper: no gunshot, no living

months in exile.
You fall back asleep.

Market Day at Koundjourou

Beating drum and two men,
drunk or driven mad: one drums

the lambskin head, the other
parades a staff veneered

with human oil, raises it
up and down like

a marching band director,
crooning his neck forward

then back, up, down—
sky to shoulders.

On the offbeat, he
lets out a war yell:

the music he feels
through drumbeat,

the unheard music
of the empty river

and market stalls
abandoned in drought days,

a song of loneliness
as a crowd circles you

asking with their distance
what it is that fills your lungs.

Downpour

after CD Wright

Where are you going when the sand-encased clouds come rolling?
Where are you going?
Where are you going when the alleyways rush with runoff?
Where
        are you going

when the sandpiper preens in the nabakh tree?
When the scorpion scurries among rooted rocks?
When the donkey foal lies down in the rutted road,
                                where

are you when the farmer finishes his last till
and the market truck takes him to Koundjourou?
Are you there where the madman and his friend
beat the goatskin drum and raise the gumwood staff
to the unheard music in their rhythmic hearts

while the millet mill pounds away afternoon
and guests gather to drink kissaar water
(so sweet, so bitter)? Do you remember
the nurse who brought you the clouded cup,
frozen from the desert dispensary freezer?

Or the horizon rain that chased your truck
over hours from Ngora to Amjamena, lightning
flashing through the risen skydust?

Do you remember how your friend messaged
you, called you
              ya mawadir?

Do you remember how he asked once more
if you would come back

                if you ever considered

coming back
        before he writes in text-speak French

tu es ou—
              you are
where?

Beqaa Valley, Lebanon

Already the camp has flooded twice—valley rain
    striking tarp tents and arms within,

rain melting into a rug or if lucky
    landing in a bowl set out to collect
                the swell

outside which pools by chairs, between tents
    and men and women wake to find their children

half-submerged,
           mattresses on floor seeped through

with the valley's sludge. Tomorrow
    in the sudden sun, mattresses will dry,

families will gather over tea glasses,
    a faded television in the corner will buzz

white noise
           to haze over the new life and sing
    back the old mundane before

the bombs fell. This television song slowly drips back
    the laughter—slowly saps back the life,

and for a moment, the questions of the dripping
    are forgotten: whether your papers will stay dry

before the army checks them, whether you should
    cross
           back into the war realm that birthed you

or cross over to a country you can't yet name.
    There is no forecast for this—no directions

for when the clouds
                    cumulate in the mountain cedars,
    for when they creep past the barbed wire checkpoints

for when the clouds settle down among the tents
    so thick there is no way to tell day from night.

Origins

Sky dark when she goes to work
and dark when she returns, Fatima
picks her kids up from school

and picks her groceries up late
and picks herself up when the length
of day wears her. Her boys make faces

and talk with strangers, and they don't know
the face of their father or fathers,
knowing only to eat, sleep, wake

the bus will get you soon,
come in the dinner gets cold,
don't play ball in jeans on wet grass—

the stain will not come out. *It's all right,*
it's all right, she still sings at night,
folding laundry to the tune of a Bantu-

laced language and hoping that her children
will hear her as they sleep and wake up
speaking anything but English.

Cable Guy

Holding two cable wires loosely,
he tells me, *This year I'll be forty.*

His grip tightens, remembering
the coils of suicide vests

and the thick copper rope of an IED
on a road outside Mosul. *I weighed 213*

when they checked me in. His steel
eyes follow the neighbor's boy

biking along the sidewalk. *I woke up*
weighing 130 in a Kansas hospital.

A few houses down, a mower stutters
to life before dying. He tells me

the woman he married after he returned
littered their bathroom with needles

before she left him, and now he checks
his phone hoping for a text from his little boy.

He ups the saturation on the television
until the image comes in clean,

colors rich like the world.
Next, he tosses the remote

to the couch, the same way
he might discard a clip

before reloading. He treads his boots
out the back door, shakes off the alley

sand as he steps into his truck and looks
at me, focuses his eyes—*Welcome,*

he says, *welcome home.*

Midwest Elegy

Not wheat fields but screens:
televisions and the dull glow
of gamers in their bedrooms.

The porches lit with emerald bulbs
host no humans. Even the towns sulk
like the empty ribs of roadkill.

Brick storefronts—the empty cathedrals
of drug and general stores—
sink with the slow gnaw
of methamphetamine.

To others this is just a pit stop,
a place to piss and purchase energy
drinks for the next century of miles.

To a few this place is the destination—
each of us wonders why it is here
we have made our bed in the shadow
of life, a land where death sulks
closer with every highway mile.

Old Man Watching *Dunkirk*

When he stood
his knees shook,

shoulders bending in
the light of the credits,

letters streaming like eyes
at a memorial

scrolling names—
those who've crafted

a narrative we might enter.
There aren't many left

to remind us
never to go back.

Not many left to say,
I've seen what

hatred can do.
Not many like

this old man
ghosted against

a fading screen—
he was the last

to leave the theater.

Protest Confession

I drove right by them—
group of twenty-odd

transplants like me
standing at the corner

of a Red Lobster solemnly
holding picket signs up

as prayers to the highway
red light I was stopped at

when I studied these souls over
my shoulder: masked voices

laboring in the Texas sun,
unsure of the street corner

or the trucks pounding gas
into their engines to shoot

by faster. The light still red,
my eyes sidetracked

suddenly by the man
in the pickup next to me.

Our eyes met then cast
away—afraid of each other,

afraid of each other's
guilt. With the light green,

we both gunned on, gone
in an exhaust cloud

we left the protesters
to breathe in.

The Mechanic Gives Advice

Go ahead and kick it off cruise and coast
past the "No Jake Brakes" sign and old folks'
home named after the Presbyterians as if
each resident was always destined to be there.
Dissect the city in a single stoplight, two grids
divided by Main or Broadway, and race
the old truck-hatted man who wobbles
on his bicycle balancing a fallen tree
branch in his lap past the frosted glass
of the pharmacy and the bells hanging
from the bars of the post office:
they will know your entry. It will sound
like Christmas for a minute, long enough
for you to stand in line. And they will know
your leaving. Know it just like all the houses
on Main that watch you pass through
from one end to the other, quicker
than it takes their microwaves to chime.

Reincarnations

last night I remembered

during duskweight

all my past lives

in a rusted-out truck

laden with smoke

the one I rode around for a half hour

a cookfire coming across

all the way out to the rows around

the still face of the town's lake

trying to hear the music again

amid corn stalks birthed under

the arched building I thought a church but proved

waterwheels all the way to

my past lives in the silo shadow

some farmer's house

the blacktop that stops

lit by the only gas station open

becomes a dirt road

tires fishtailing

an unlit house where

I knock at the unlit house

my past life

that lives and waits for me

lives and waits for me

III

*I do not know how to come closer to God
except by standing where a world is ending
for one man.*

—Christian Wiman

God Particle

Misnomer. That the question of how we got here,
what force propelled us into existence,

why we collided together, formed into being
like a missing link, could ever be answered

with a single spark. No, it is not the answer:
higgs boson, particle hiding behind atomic

forces we can't quite put a finger on just yet.
It is not the source, not the solution,

though perhaps it is the method—this hurtling
of particles through a tube underneath

the Alps, waiting as if for lightning to strike.
We used to say the spheres could move,

that they existed, were turned like wheels
by divine hands, so maybe this is a consideration

hypothesized through the experiment itself:
this proof that propelling microscopic particles

in a mile-long tube is not so much different
than us wandering an atmospheric bubble—

another mind throwing us, our lives, our planet,
through the dark wide vacuum of space.

To the Stars Through Difficulty

Somewhere in the fever dream
of loss your hatchback hums
down the dark highway swell
until distinguished from one shadow
is the next—a whole backdrop
of blinks, wind turbine lights
like eyes burning the night,
more lighthouse than warning
light beckoning you into the land
of the living and the lived.
The next day you will box up
another life yet again, prepare it
for the unknown beyond just an address.
But for now: these humming miles,
these whispered farewells, and
the mind's ever-turning—
how do you learn to lose a land
you are just beginning to love?

Equinox

This oil forest, pine field city
wakes into spring having never
lost its young leaves or lingering
morning fog. But some days I wake
slower than the rest and find a tree
diseased like the stretching oak
that died on my arrival—now shedding
limbs like leaves, bark like pieces
of a body to bury in the earth. One day
I woke and found myself divorced
and drove north along Estes
taking note as always of the faded
ranch-style home, squat and derelict
among the derricks and tractor
stores, its shutters dangling an invitation
to pull it to pieces and start from studs,
but no one does—acres imminently
awaiting a government contract
to bulldoze, begin again with something
wholly different, leveled acres so
immaculately green you never
knew what grew there before.

Poem

Here and now and not yet—
like a child in the everpresent,
cradling in the palm a rock
and finding it a world.

After the Miscarriage

I heard the birds as I left the house
the next day—there were clouds of them

all up and down the street, speaking
so thick their songs were a curtain

of freedom. The curtain lifted
as I came close, gone to blanket

some other street with a thousand voices
screaming life life life.

On Reading Wiesel's *Night*

You were right—
God is hanging here

on the gallows.
Here breathing in

poison gas,
walking under

the Auschwitz
welcome sign—

Work sets you
free. Here he is

huddled in the corner
of an overcrowded

cabin, sipping
from a cup

soup the color
of blood.

I won't believe
in a God

who is only
watching

the suffering,
who isn't being

killed alongside them
slowly, infinitely.

Before the Ultrasound

If a boy then all my dreams
of the girl   will be for the lost
one she will never come
waving sunhair never
speak *Dad* never wonder
in slow afternoon what it is
that makes starling clouds
twist and lift never say *Love*
you head nested tight never
walk with me by the gully
pine cones crunching
underneath *They sound*
like little bones   O my vision
of you little one you who never
grew beyond the size of a tree
seed you who never wondered
at the birds but chose instead
to join them.

Sunday Afternoons are for Mourning

You were our sunray,
our shard of star,

held in the hand
for only an hour.

The Thousand Ways You've Wounded

Think of the fracture in a home's foundation.
The crack that shifts and splits roof, lets in

rain and rot and root. Think of the smoke screen
concealing a pine forest conflagration—

fallen trunks cloaked in ash and ember.
Think of the scorched earth of every row

all the way from root to road to horizon.

Think of the sky and the heart
and their many chambers:

all full of holes, all drained
of moisture—
                    chambers emptied
of life leading to life elsewhere.

Think of the thousand ways you've wounded.
Think of disfigured earth, every fracture.

Think of what is left behind:
each earth hurt, each wind violation—

no patch of earth that does not know you,
no blade of grass that does not grieve you.

The Pastor Walks Me Through His House

See the beams we gathered ten hands to hang,
triangular trusses the rain threatened

to keep grounded? See the old oak claimed
from the deserted farmhouse, weathered

by earth and storms? We'll turn this warped
roof into three attic rooms and the stairs

coming up we'll shift, replace with solid steps—
not the ones you can see through.

When you drove in, did you get stuck in the mud ruts
running from the farm road to the barn?

Did you see the thousand white water birds come
roosting just outside of town—the ones that will leave

in a cloud just as they've come? Come rest a while
on these paint cans and fill me in, but watch out

for that hole there between the boards—
if you fall, you'll fall clean through.

Complex

Even when I wake I'm sinning
Even when your voice wakes me I'm sinning

Even when I don't hear you I'm sinning
Even when I lie alone I'm sinning

Along the pine root trail I'm sinning
In the shade of the post oak I'm sinning

Even when the world opens to sun
searing the lake's ridges

and the paths we walked
                                    I'm still sinning

I'm sinning when I think of you
and when I don't I'm sinning

Sinning when I sit across from a face
her face I'm sinning

I'm sinning even when I don't remember
or when I try to, imperfectly, with love

and always still while sinning.

Some Lumber

Some lumber is too long
for the eighteen-wheeler.

It has to be piled on, draped
past the truck bed

sagging down like a finger ready
to drag a line through sand.

Wrapped with a red ribbon,
some lumber hangs

defeated, lies still like the acres
out past McCann

once so full, now a horizon
sightline. Some lumber falls

where it will, not where
it was, leaning uprooted

against other pines
still sapped and veining.

Not yet a downed tree but
no longer living. Some lumber

waits for the next wind
to send it to the earth,

regardless of whether
it was heard, sheltered life,

or was wanted.

Future Self

"In my age of grief, I am unknowing everything."
                                    – Melanie Rae Thon

Fear of the absent text
of the unread bed of the unknown
home of the single plate of the one-
serving meal of no answer when
you call no come here caress
no one to say you look like
the shadow of the shuttered
blinds no one to combine
clothes with for a load
no toothbrush to pair
in a plastic cup of fear
the future memory rid
the future of the new you
always an unmaking
never something made.

Dog Logic

My stray paws the door to go out to go in
to my bedroom, get fed, and curl into
his pile of rags. He's refused anything
better—shredding dog beds into foam
shards that take me months to gather.
In the mornings his teeth carry favorite
toys into the yard to display them
to the leaves, toys not buried but left
like the *lawn ornament* the shelter workers
said he had become—why he has those
bug bite scars under his ears, why weeks
went by before he knew my voice so that now
he can't bear for me to be in another room.
When my stray comes to nudge me
with his leather nose, it's not to be scratched
as to be seen—to bait me into a chase,
to pull away just so I can call him back.

Hymn

Christ is the lover walking home at night
along the street of elation. Christ is the boy

picking shells along the Delaware shore
until he finds a gleaming shark tooth.

Christ is the cloud of rain a man sees miles away,
enveloping him slowly across the hours.

Christ is the light-crested Mediterranean
waves, prism of mint-tea as it is poured,

Levant wind—lull between summer
monsoon and winter drought—the waking dream,

birth into life oozing across forehead
like baptismal water, the voice that arrests you

that says to you, a word, the word.

Suspension of (Dis)belief

as in forgetting the way in which
you were raised, as in forsaking
every good word you've read
in the Good Book—as if your
actions now would be reactions—
this is not abandonment

but something else entirely,
more like the feeling a butterfly
must have when breaking from
its spit-wad nest, first freeing
a technicolor wing and then
another, first the twisting,
the breaking before the flutter—

more like the prominence
of an art display at a museum
when you first walk in: *you have
no option but to confront it.*

Something else pulls the weight,
pulls and yearns and lets go
like the ten-story-tall crane
you see on your way to work:
swiveling and lifting steel like
a toothpick. It asks of you
before you ask of it like when
a hang-glider runs headlong
to the cliff edge not knowing
 if the wind will carry him
to the horizon's end

or suspend its given gust.
Before suspension, there
must be belief undeniably
in the things that are, belief
that another sits somewhere
watching over, pulling strings.

Visitations

You and me mimic
the turtle who
grunt steps
across the soccer
field wary-eyed
with eyes deep
as the lake basin
he's flopped his way from where
the heron we followed
ghosted across surface
your sapling finger
tracing the wake
of the bird's feathers.
We reach for the roots
knobbed like elbow
bones unearthed
out of the shore's
sand, we brush
against the willow
fingertips cradling
these minutes
gifted to us
then taken when
I return you
to your mother,
and watch from the curb
as the door closes,
tracing the signs of life
you leave in your wake.

Children

after chewing
foliage

the colobus
sleeps chin down

down the path
from the bear den

where the two
brothers slumber

against the glass
division

arm in arm
wombed in shade

under the deep pines
throughout where

even the antelopes
test out the path

together near
the rails

and the onlookers
who watch

without words
this whole herd

How We Come to Language

How we come to language, the little ones,
testing the percussive syllables

of *ba* and *na* as if reciting the letters of Arabic.
No wonder our letters were crafted around

first words, universal syllables, echoes like those
for a father—*dada, baba, papa.*

From these beginning steps come
the foray into words, synapses

stretching syntax in the same way
the world expands, becomes real,

becomes something to be navigated
in baby shoes, babbling all the while

with what my brother called *creature
language* when he watched me speak.

Our DNA is to name: how we call the sky
the sky, how we name the dirt rimming

our fingernails. How those shadows of pets,
our first lessons in death, become the zoo

made flesh to dwell among us.
In the beginning was the word *wonder*

one friend told me—what we whisper
to ourselves as we watch the little ones

turn their tongues toward infinity.

Paradiso, Canto **XXXIII**

My speech will be short like the memory of a child
   who still drinks from his mother's breast: not that
   the living light was simple—it never really changed—

but as I gained the strength to look more and more,
   the single image, the sole object, began to take shape
   as I myself was shaped: clearness of light, profound

and beyond, merged into three circles, each with another
   color (or were they the same?). Two reflected one on
   another, rainbow on rainbow, the third fire-breathed

from their layers. *Speech fails to express, words a spark*
   of what was! These lines can't even be called "little"
   in comparison! Eternal Light, you live in yourself,

you know yourself, and—both known and knowing—
   you love and are pleased in you! The circling, thus made,
   was a shaft of light around you and yet your own reflection

all the same. The more I looked at it, seemingly, it was my own
   likeness in its light, in its color like a stroke of paint.
   I couldn't take my eyes away, like a mathematician trying

to make a square of a circle, a circle of a square, never finding
   the formula he needs (so he thinks until his head hurts,
   this was how I felt staring into this strangeness).

If only I could see how the image fitted the circle,
   how it fit there at all, embodied yet not, wanting
   a place as much as I—the wings of my mind could

not fly to that place, the place of understanding. But
for a flash that made it clear: my power failed
the highest thought, and my will, given energy

to turn again, became like a wheel revolved by love—
that love, you know, that moves the sun and stars.

Reading *Velveteen Rabbit*

Really? You've never read it?
Then as a joke, you opened the cover,

wove the tale with your playful voice,
speaking as if to a child, and I listened

with a lover's ears. The rabbit turned
from fabric to life with your language.

And I wondered. And I believed.
In the divorce, you came and took

the book from the shelf, nested
it in a box, and left. The life I had

been lit with snuffed with the close
of a door, close of a cover.

God of the Midwest

God like the leaf studs in tire-tracks across the grass.
God like the dust veil raised
from a harvester
                           chewing the stalks
until the field is lit with headlight beams.

God the God of the cement silo, sunset-stained,
and the conveyer
                           running through the night.
God like the sludge of a sinking stream
like a slinking coon
                           growling away a passerby
beneath a guard-railed bridge.

God the road that goes from blacktop
into rutted and rumbled dirt.

                           God the God the God
of a land that is a thousand miles of sameness
a thousand rows of unknowing
                           that is
a small town in a clump of trees
and the expanse that surrounds it.

Always We Begin Again

Today you could wake up and say, *It doesn't have to be complicated—*
life, that is, in the way a forest overtakes the scourge of the machine.

Eventually, the scar will be covered first by high grasses and flowering
weeds, then shoulder high pines that spine their way to the leaf ceiling.

Life, you could say, could be like that. A regrowth, something
the whole forest seems to agree upon, beginning the moment after

the metal teeth carve a wound. Life could be like that, and love.
Love—the way years from now you will look down the path

the machine took and never know that once this was the way
the humans went, blistering their way, metal teeth dripping sap.

Notes

The epigraphs at the beginning of each section are taken from the following: *Victims of a Map: A Bilingual Anthology of Arabic Poetry by Adonis* (Saqi Books 2008), *Selected Poems* by Gwendolyn Brooks (Harper Perennial 2006), *Every Riven Thing* by Christian Wiman (Farrar, Straus & Giroux 2011), and the interview "Creating a World in Which Everything that Dies is Mourned" with Victoria Chang in Electric Literature.

"Bury" is for Ellis Purdie. "In a parallel universe" is modeled after a poem by Julie Moore. "To the Stars Through Difficulty" is a translation of the state motto of Kansas. "Future Self" contains an epigraph from Melanie Rae Thon's essay "The Gospel of Grief & Grace & Gratitude" in AGNI. "Hymn" is for Li-Young Lee. "Always We Begin Again" takes its title from St. Benedict.

About the Author

Aaron Brown is the author of the poetry collection, *Acacia Road*, winner of the 2016 Gerald Cable Book Award (Silverfish Review Press, 2018) and of the memoir, *Less Than What You Once Were* (Unsolicited Press, 2022). He has received Pushcart Prize and Best of the Net nominations, and his work has been published in magazines such as *Prairie Schooner, Michigan Quarterly Review, Image, World Literature Today online, Waxwing,* and *Transition,* among others. He is a contributing editor for Windhover. Brown grew up in Chad and now lives in Texas, where he is an assistant professor of English and directs the writing center at LeTourneau University. He holds an MFA from the University of Maryland. Follow his work at www.aaronbrownwriter.com.